good night, God

Sleepytime Prayers for Children

good night, God

Bernadette McCarver Snyder

ave maria press   Notre Dame, Indiana

©2000 by Ave Maria Press, Inc.

International Standard Book Number: 0-87793-940-3

Cover, text design, and illustrations by Katherine Robinson Coleman

Printed and bound in the United States of America.

Library of Congress Cataloging-in-Publication Data

Snyder, Bernadette McCarver.
        Good night God : sleepytime prayers for children /
Bernadette McCarver Snyder.
                p.   cm.
                Summary: Suggested activities which engage the reader's
                imagination accompany prayers for bedtime.
                ISBN 0-87793-940-3 (pbk.)
                1. Bedtime prayers. 2. Children--Prayer-books and
                devotions--English. [1. Prayers. 2. Bedtime.] I. Title.
BV283.B43 S69 2000
242'.82--dc21   00-008462
                                           CIP

I dedicate this book to all the girls and boys who look at the world through imagination-colored glasses, who know how to have just-pretend adventures wherever they are—but who also can look at the REAL world and find wonder and excitement there too.

I especially dedicate it to

Matthew Joseph Snyder

and

William Daniel Snyder.

Contents

Autumn

School Bus, Pumpkin Patch, and Trick-or-Treat Time ~ 50

Strike up the band . . . School daze . . . Give me s'more . . . Trick or treat! . . . Invisible me . . . Choo-choo and clickety-clack . . . Pilgrims and pumpkins . . . Zippy-dee-do-wah . . . On the shelf . . . Once upon a time . . .

Wintertime

Snow, Blow, Ho-Ho-Ho Time ~ 70

Brrr—the polar bear . . . Who's in that igloo? . . . Who, whooo? . . . Blastoff! . . . A dark and stormy night . . . Me and my pillow . . . Going underground . . . Whose birthday is this? . . . The wise, looong journey . . . Sleeping out or over . . .

Easy, Please-y Prayers ~ 90

Introduction

Mmmm . . . nitey-nite time . . . time to snooze and cruise into dreamland. But AFTER you have that last drink of water and BEFORE you close your eyes and put out the light, it's time to say some good-night prayers.

Maybe you have some favorite prayers you say EVERY night.

Maybe you like to say "God bless . . . " prayers—like . . .

> God bless Mama and Daddy . . . Aunt Philadelphia and Uncle Piddy-Paddy . . . All the giraffelos in the zoo and all the sneezer-weezers who say kerchoo . . . All the boys and girls in Somewheresville and all the tiddleywinks in Nowheresville.

Maybe you like to say the "Our Father" or a special prayer your Grandma taught you.

All of those are VERY good ways to say good night.

Now here's another way . . . some "imagination" prayers and some "let's pretend" prayers . . .

to help you think about all the fun and wun-derful things you can talk about to God.

Just remember . . .

whatever you do or say,
a prayer is the very best way
to end the day.

Springtime

Bloom and Bunny, Jelly Bean, and Green Time

The green submarine . . .

Tonight would be a good night to IMAGINE . . . to get way down under the covers and "just pretend" to be inside a submarine. . . .

There's room to move around in here—but not much! And there are no windows so I can't see outside. I can look through the periscope which is like a telescope that can look up and over the water. But I still can't see very much. The big green submarine is like a big green fish, sliding through the water, quietly, silently. No one on TOP of the water knows I am UNDER the water. But being inside the submarine is NOT like being inside a FISH. There are lots of dials and switches to run the submarine and there are bunks where you can sleep and a kitchen where you COULD eat a tunaFISH sandwich. A submarine is like an underwater house! But tonight, I don't think I'd like to sleep in an underwater house, so I'll hit the button and turn the dial that will bring the green submarine from below to above water!

Dear God, you made LOTS of underwater houses—all those curved and colored shells that are the homes of underwater creatures. Some of your shells are as fancy in design as a fancy people house! You must have been very busy when you made all the wonderful things that are on the earth and under the ocean.

So thank you and good night.

Go fly a kite...

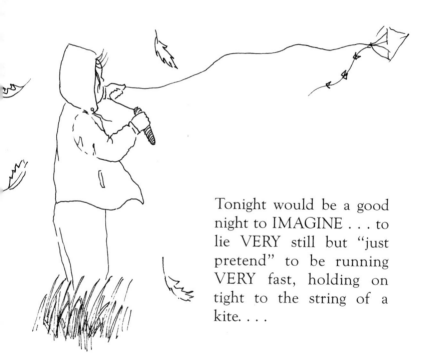

Tonight would be a good night to IMAGINE . . . to lie VERY still but "just pretend" to be running VERY fast, holding on tight to the string of a kite. . . .

The wind is blowing just right today and my kite is flying higher and higher. I have to run fast to keep up with it. And then I have to give the kite more string. And then I have to stop and watch where the kite goes. It doesn't just go high. It goes this way and then that way, running with the wind. It looks like it's playing hide-and-seek or peekaboo with the clouds. I think my kite is having a good time today. And I'm having a good time too!

Dear Jesus, I guess you didn't have a kite when you were a little boy. I guess nobody had thought to make one yet. I wonder who got the idea to make the very FIRST kite. It sure was a good idea. It was probably YOUR idea and you put it into somebody's head because you knew it would be fun for kids to fly kites. You know things like that since you were a kid yourself. And I'm so glad.

So thank you and good night.

Splish-splash . . .

Tonight would be a good night to IMAGINE . . . to snuggle down, relax, and "just pretend" it's a rainy day. . . .

I'm looking out the window and I see the rain starting. At first, it's just a few little drops and then the rain pours harder and harder until it looks like a big bucket of water dropped out of the sky—right against my window. I like to watch the little raindrops running down the window-pane like they're playing follow the leader. And I like to watch the BIG rains too and imagine I'm watching a waterfall in a rain forest. The only time I DON'T like rain is when we're going on a picnic. But I know we NEED the rain because nothing on earth can LIVE without water—not even me! I'm REALLY glad for rain in the spring-time because the new leaves on the trees and bushes and flowers are probably REALLY thirsty for a good drink of water.

Dear God, thank you for making water to fill up the lakes and rivers and oceans—AND to fill up thirsty plants and people. Sometimes before I go to sleep I get so thirsty, I REALLY want a drink of water. And I'm glad we have water faucets right in our house so I don't have to wait for it to rain to get a drink!

So thank you and good night.

Over the rainbow...

Tonight would be a good night to IMAGINE . . . to lie on the pillow and look up and "just pretend" to be looking for something in the sky. . . .

Sometimes, after it has stopped raining, I look up in the sky and I look for a rainbow. And sometimes I spot one—a rainbow full of colors. Even if I can't find a rainbow, I can look around and see that the WHOLE WORLD is full of colors—and I'm glad. I wooonder but I don't THINK a black and white watermelon would taste as good as a red and green one does. I don't think a garden full of only black and white flowers would look as pretty as one with lots of colors. And I don't think white clouds in a WHITE sky would be as much fun to watch as white clouds in a BLUE sky!

Dear Lord, I'm glad you made red strawberries and blue birds, golden kitty-cats and purple grapes, brown puppies and green grass. But I'm glad you also made some black and white things—like black-and-white striped zebras, white snowflakes and white swans—and BLACK clouds that bring rain when we need it.

So thank you and good night.

A slinky kitty...

Tonight would be a good night to IMAGINE . . . to pull up the covers, to get comfy and "just pretend" to be playing with a kittycat. . . .

Tonight I AM a kittycat, hiding and watching. I'm sneaking up on another mysterious kittycat who acts like his relatives—the tigers. He's always sneaking around the yard or the house, hunting! I don't know what he's hunting for—and maybe he doesn't either—but he slinks about like a pirate searching for buried treasure. His eyes can see when it's black and dark and his whiskers guide him through narrow spaces so he can sneak up and pounce when I don't expect it. Uh oh! Here he comes now. But what's this? I guess he got tired of hunting because he just wants to curl up near me and cuddle and purr—and probably go to sleep.

Dear Jesus, it's true. Sometimes I AM like a cat. I like to play hide-and-seek and sneak around, hiding or hunting. And sometimes I like to cuddle up near someone I love too. And sometimes I get very tired and need to sleep—even when I don't WANT to sleep. Tonight I'm very glad that I have a nice warm place where I can sleep, all curled up like a kittycat.

So thank you and good night.

Wishing on a star . . .

Tonight would be a good night to IMAGINE . . . to wiggle around and find just the right spot to be comfy and "just pretend" to be looking up at a sky full of stars. . . .

The stars are so bright and so mysterious. They blink, they wink. They sparkle like diamonds. "Star light . . . star bright . . . I wish a wish I wish tonight." What shall I wish for tonight? Should I wish to grow up to be a famous scientist who discovers a cure for a terrible disease? Should I wish to be an explorer who travels to strange lands and makes maps of places very few have ever been before? Should I wish my family would get a new house or a new car? Should I wish for a new bicycle or a new toy? Or tonight maybe I'll just wish for a hot fudge sundae for lunch tomorrow.

Dear Lord, I know that wishing on a star won't make wishes come true. But it's a beginning! It makes me THINK about what I might wish for if I could have ANYthing. Sometimes I wish for little things—like ice cream or candy. Sometimes I'm selfish and wish for something that I don't really need—like a silly toy I saw on TV. But sometimes I start to think about what I would wish to be when I grow up. I'm too young to KNOW that just yet, but I can think about it and I can pray that you'll help me work and do all the right things to make my wishes come true someday.

So thank you and good night.

A bright idea . . .

Tonight would be a good night to IMAGINE . . . to pull up the covers, turn down the lights, and "just pretend" to be a light bulb. . . .

Be careful when you get near me—I'm little and I'm made out of glass so I can break. But I'm GLAD I'm made the way I am! I am very important and I am powerful! Everybody is happy to see me when I light up. Everybody NEEDS my light at night to walk through a room without bumping into something. Tonight I'll shine my light so a little boy can look at a book. I'll shine in a big stadium so a lot of people can watch a ballgame. I'll go out to the airport and light the way for a jet to roar down the runway and land safely. I LIKE being a light bulb. I'm glad somebody had the bright idea to make me just the way I am.

Dear God, thank you for making ME just the way I am too. I guess I'm like the light bulb because I'm little too. I'm not made of glass although I AM kinda breakable. But I am important and powerful too! You gave me legs so I can run and help people. You gave me eyes and ears and a voice so I can notice all the great things you put in the world—and then tell others about them. I can light up a room for somebody by giving out hugs and giggles instead of complaining and whining. I can help my friends by being a good sport when we play games. I can do LOTS of things.

So thank you and good night.

Up, up
in the air . . .

Tonight would be a good night to IMAGINE . . . to jiggle and jaggle around until I find the BEST spot in the bed and then "just pretend" to be a bird. . . .

I can feel myself flying high into the sky, looking down on a snow-topped mountain or on the big waves of an ocean or on the treetops of a tropical rain forest. I can fly here. I can fly there. I can fly EVERYwhere. I can hide in the leaves of a tree or I can perch on the wires of a telephone pole! I can be an eagle soaring higher and higher into the air—or I can be a tiny hummingbird flying faster and faster from flower to flower. What fun it would be to have my own pair of wings!

Dear Lord, sometimes I think I would like to be free to fly like a bird. But a bird has to live outside in the cold or the rain or even in a storm—but I get to live INside. And a bird has to SEARCH for food every day, but I get to eat good food with my family. When I think about that, I think I am lucky to be me—especially since I can pretend to be a bird whenever I want and pretend to fly wherever I want. Birds don't have an imagination—but I do!

So thank you and good night.

The good "NEWS"...

Tonight would be a good night to IMAGINE . . . to fluff up the pillow and "just pretend" that the pillow is as fluffy as a bunny rabbit's tail. . . .

Here comes Peter Cottontail, hopping down the bunny trail . . . because when it's springtime, it's time for Easter. Mr. Cottontail has a big new bow tied around his neck because everybody likes to wear something NEW at Eastertime. The trees are wearing new leaves and some of the bushes and gardens have bright new flowers. A lot of the people are wearing something new or nice. And some of us are going to an Easter egg hunt. I wonder how many eggs I will find. I wonder if I will find more than ANYbody else in the whole world! If I do, that will be a big surprise!

Dear Jesus, I think Easter is fun, but I also know that it is YOUR holiday. I know we celebrate with NEW things because it was on Easter when you surprised the whole world by doing something new! On Good Friday you died on the cross, but on Easter Sunday, you came right back again, full of NEW life. Nobody else in the world could do that! Now we know you did that so that when we die, we will get NEW life in heaven too! And that's really GOOD NEWS. I hope you have a happy time with all those people in heaven, dear Jesus, and for every Easter egg I find, I will think of you—and the great Easter surprise you gave the world!

So thank you and good night.

My magic pajamas...

Tonight would be a good night to IMAGINE . . . to relax the muscles in my neck, my arms, my knees, my toes, and "just pretend" to be wearing magic pajamas. . . .

It's amazing! It's fantastic! It's magic! These pajamas are making my muscles grow. My arms are getting so strong I could hang on to a vine and fly through the trees like Tarzan. Now the muscles in my legs are getting so big I could leap a tall building in a single bound like Superman. Wait, wait! Now my fingers are twitching and I think they've learned how to play the piano so well I could play in a concert. Now my voice is changing so maybe I could sing opera or be a rock star. And I can feel my brain growing and turning into a genius brain. Wow! These magic pajamas have made a whole new me. But who will I be when I take them off???

Dear God, I know pajamas can't be magic, but YOU are better than magic. Magic is a trick, but YOU are real. I know when I take off my pajamas, I will still be me—with the arms and legs and fingers and voice and brain that YOU gave me. I know you gave me talents too. I don't know yet what my best talents are, but whatever they are, I know if I really WANT to do something, it won't happen by magic. It will happen if I study hard and work hard and pray hard. And I know I don't HAVE to be a super somebody. I just need to be the BEST I can be—the way you made me to be and want me to be.

So thank you and good night.

Summertime

Lemonade, Lollipops, Sprinklers, and Sparklers Time

Lemonade in the shade . . .

Tonight would be a good night to IMAGINE . . . to feel totally limp and "just pretend" to be under a tree, swinging in a hammock. . . .

Swinging left to right . . . left to right. I am warm and lazy and limp as a noodle as I swing and sway, left to right, in the hammock that is hanging between two tall trees. The sunshine feels good, the shade of the tree feels good, and I am drinking a glass of lemonade that tastes good. I am watching a spider weaving a fancy web on the side of the patio. The spider is very busy. I am not. I am watching a butterfly going from flower to flower, sipping nectar. The butterfly is very busy. I am not. I hear the neighbor cutting the grass. He is very busy. I am not. Sometimes I LIKE to be very busy—running, skating, biking, playing games. Sometimes I am bored if I am not busy. Today I am not.

Dear Jesus, today I just want to be quiet. I want to think about the sunshine and the trees and the spider and the butterfly and my neighbor. You made them all. You even made the lemons for my lemonade. And you made me. Everything and everyone you made is so different.

So thank you and good night.

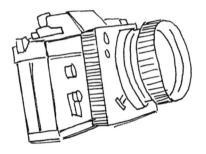

Smile! ...

Tonight would be a good night to IMAGINE . . . to curl up in bed and "just pretend" to be a photographer, crouched down to take a picture. . . .

I like my new camera and I came to the zoo today to use it. I am kneeling down trying to get a good picture of a lion in a cage. I wish he would open his mouth in a big roar, but he won't even look at me. I think I'll photograph the seal instead. He's flapping his flippers and splashing water all over. That should make a real good picture. And now I see the monkeys. They must LIKE to pose for pictures. They are climbing and smiling and making faces. Next I'll aim my camera at some people. I can take a picture of some kids. They are climbing and smiling and making faces too! I got some really good pictures today!

Dear Jesus, do you remember when someone invented the first camera? Before then, I guess nobody had a family album. I'm glad WE have a family album. I like to look at pictures of me when I was a baby. I like to look at wedding pictures and really old pictures when people wore funny clothes and hats. I wish I could see a real picture of YOU, Jesus—not what some artist THINKS you looked like but a photograph of what you REALLY looked like. Someone told me that the Bible is like YOUR family album. It doesn't have any photographs, but it DOES have some really good stories—and I like to "picture" those stories in my mind.

So thank you and good night.

Around the world . . .

Tonight would be a good night to IMAGINE . . .
to lie back, get very quiet, and "just pretend" to
be traveling around the world. . . .

I have heard that since the world is round, it isn't always nighttime in other countries when it's nighttime where I live. When I'm getting ready to go to sleep, a little boy or girl somewhere else in the world—like maybe in Zanzibar or Timbuktu—is just waking up! When I am waking up, people somewhere else are just going to sleep! When I am having breakfast, people somewhere else are having dinner. The earth is an exciting planet. Things on the earth are always moving, always growing, always changing—just like I am!

Dear Lord, now that I have on my pajamas, I wonder who is getting dressed to go to school. I wonder who is eating breakfast or thinking about what games to play or what books to read. I know one thing, Lord—you are with me HERE and you are with them THERE. And that is a very nice thing to know.

So thank you and good night.

Chasing clouds . . .

Tonight would be a good night to IMAGINE . . . to lie flat on my bed and look straight up and "just pretend" to be chasing clouds. . . .

Oh, look at that big white cloud coming this way. It looks like a white elephant! And the elephant is pulling a cart with his tail. And what is that in the cart? Is it a monkey? No! It's a little boy. And he's sitting next to a little girl. Or is that a giraffe? Too late. The cloud is breaking up. But wait! Here comes another cloud and it looks like a bowl of apples. No. It's a bowl of turtles. No. It's a bowl of balloons. But whoever saw a balloon in a bowl? I did! I just did! Oh, oh. Here comes a gray cloud. Is it full of rain? No. It's full of gray donkeys! Oh boy, I like finding pictures in pretend clouds. Maybe tomorrow afternoon, I can go out in the yard and find pictures in some REAL clouds!

Dear God, thank you for making clouds. We NEED clouds to bring us rain in the summer when the farmers are growing corn and tomatoes and potatoes—and lots of people are growing flowers. Those vegetables and flowers get thirsty for rain water. But we need clouds ALL YEAR too—in the winter, spring, and fall. And God, do you know why? So we can play games, finding pictures in the clouds! But I guess you already knew that, didn't you? Maybe that's why you MADE clouds the way you did.

So thank you and good night.

Batter up!...

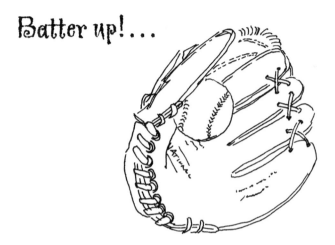

Tonight would be a good night to IMAGINE . . . to lie back real easy and "just pretend" to be at a baseball game. . . .

We have good seats and a great view of the baseball field. The grass is so green and the baseball players look great in their uniforms. Here comes my favorite batter. Will he get a home run tonight? I hope so. Strike one. Ball one. Strike two. Oh no! Three strikes and you're out. Well, maybe he'll hit that homer next time up. Hey, here comes a guy selling snacks. Yum, yum! I don't know why, but food always tastes better at a ballgame. I like to WATCH the game, but I like even better to pretend that I'M the batter on a big league team and it's my turn to bat. Here comes the ball. Look at it go. It's out of the stadium. I'm the home run star!

Dear Jesus, it would be great to be a star, but it's fun to be a watcher too. And when you're a watcher, you don't have to be so worried about being up at bat next. Maybe some day I will play on a team and be a star, but maybe I won't and that's OK too. Either way, I know the important thing about a ballgame— or any game—is to play your hardest, play fair, and play to win. But if I DON'T win, I'll try to be a good loser. Since I don't LIKE to lose, please help me remember, Jesus, to always play by YOUR rules.

So thank you and good night.

Swinging and sliding . . .

Tonight would be a good night to IMAGINE . . . to lie back and relax and "just pretend" to be playing at a playground. . . .

It's fun to swing on the swings, slide down the slide, and go UUUP and DOWWN on the seesaw. But sometimes when I'm at the playground, it is NOT fun. That's when somebody starts to tease me. Or somebody bigger picks on me. Or somebody makes fun of the way I'm playing. It's not easy being nice to somebody who is NOT being nice to you. But most of the time most of the kids are nice and it's great fun to run and climb and hollerrrrr! It's OK to holler louder outside than inside! And there's more room to run too!

Dear Jesus, you were little once too so maybe you know how hard it can be when somebody picks on you. I know some people picked on you when you were grown-up, so maybe they teased you when you were little too. Help me to know what to do when there's a bad time at the playground. Help me to know if it's braver to shove back or talk back—or just walk away. Help me to know when it's time to ask a grownup for help—and which grownup to ask. And thank you, Jesus, for letting us have playgrounds. Some children never get to play on one. There are only a few times when something at a playground makes me mad or sad. All the rest of the time, playgrounds are sooooo much fun!

So thank you and good night.

Building sandcastles ...

Tonight would be a good night to IMAGINE . . .
to kick off the covers and "just pretend" to be on
a warm sunny beach by the ocean. . . .

The waves are roaring in and the water is very
cool but the sand is warm and squiggly under my

toes. Some friends and I are building a sandcastle, filling buckets with sand, then piling up the sand and shaping it to look like castle rooms and look-out towers. Our castle has a moat to keep out any bad guys. We are using little shovels and sticks and decorating the castle with stones and shells we found on the beach. It's fun to imagine what it would be like to live in a castle—to wear a royal robe made of velvet and a crown made of gold and jewels. But real castles look like they might be so big you could get lost in one and you wouldn't have any next-door neighbors to play with. So I think I like SANDcastles better.

Dear Jesus, it's fun to have day-dreams and imagine what it would be like to live in a castle or travel in a strange foreign land or shoot to the moon or discover a new planet, but it's nice to come home to my own toys, my own family, and my own bed where I can day-dream OR night-dream.

So thank you and good night.

Sailing away ...

Tonight would be a good night to IMAGINE . . .
to sink back into the pillow and "just pretend" to
be sailing away on a sailboat. . . .

The wind feels good on my face and it is
filling the sails so they look like big white bed
sheets floating in the air. The boat is moving fast
but not too fast—just right. There are lots of

other boats sailing around in the water and lots of birds sailing around in the air. I am sailing off like Christopher Columbus did, wondering if the world is flat or round, wondering if I will discover a new land and become a hero, or if I will fail and people will laugh at me. I sail waaaay out in the water until I can't see any land anywhere. Should I turn around and go back or should I keep sailing farther and farther awaaay?

Dear God, it was very smart of you to make the earth round so we can sail away and keep going and keep going around the world until we come back to where we started! I LIKE living on a round world. It's kinda hard to understand how the world can be round because I can stand up without falling off—but a lot of the things you made are mysterious and I LIKE mysterious things.

So thank you and good night.

A pool is cool...

Tonight would be a good night to IMAGINE . . .
to let all my muscles go limp and "just pretend"
to be floating in a swimming pool. . . .

This pool is cool. The water is cool on a hot day and the things I can do in the water are cool ways to spend a day. I can float on my back or on a blown-up raft or inner tube. I can try to swim across the pool—with waterwings or without. I can do a cannonball dive into the water. I can splash my friends and let them splash me. Summertime is watertime—time to play in a pool or run through the sprinkler at home or just sit and eat juicy, watery watermelon! I think a hot summertime is real cool.

Dear God, I'm glad you let me have summertime. I know that in different parts of the world, it can be cold most of the year, and in other parts of the world, it can be hot most of the year, but I think it's nice to have a little of each—wintertime, spring, summertime, and fall. I like that a lot.

So thank you and good night.

Let the sun shine in . . .

Tonight would be a good night to IMAGINE . . . to stretch out on top of the covers and "just pretend" to be lying in the warm sunshine. . . .

I'm watching the sun today. Oh, I'm not looking right AT the sun because that would hurt my eyes. I'm watching how the shine of the sun looks different in different parts of my yard. In one spot, the sun is so bright it looks like it could bake a cookie right on the sidewalk. Underneath the apple tree, the sun looks like yellow freckles where it peeks through the leaves and just shines in spots here and there. In the flower garden, there are some long strips of sun and some of shade because the sun shines on the tall plants and the tall plants make shade for the short plants. But all day the sun skips around the yard—peeking over the fence, hiding behind the big oak tree, jumping out from behind the tall hedge to surprise me. I think the sun likes to play just the way I do!

Dear God, I like to watch the sun. I miss it on days when there are only clouds and rain—but then, sometimes I like the clouds and the rain too. I like ALMOST everything you made, God. I'm not sure WHY you made spinach and mosquitoes, but I like just about everything else.

So thank you and good night.

Autumn

School Bus, Pumpkin Patch, and Trick-or-Treat Time

Strike up the band ...

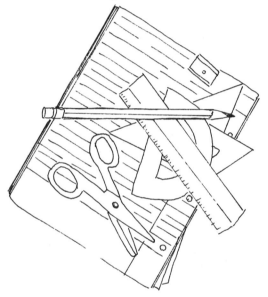

Tonight would be a good night to IMAGINE . . . to throw my shoulders back very straight and "just pretend" to be marching in a parade. . . .

The band is playing, the flags are flying, and I am marching along the street, holding my backyard shoulders very straight and keeping in step with the music. I love a parade and this is a special one—in honor of all the people who WORK. Every year, when the summer is ending and it's back-to-school time, lots of people who work all year get a day OFF when they don't have to work—and the town has a Labor Day parade to celebrate. Sometimes I stand on the sidewalk and watch the parade go by, but now I am marching and waving at all the people standing on the sidewalk watching ME go by. This is fun!

Dear Jesus, thank you for all the people who work and do ALL kinds of jobs to keep our world running—people who work in stores and restaurants, people who drive trucks and trains, people who fix streets and pick up trash, people who make toys and fly airplanes. There is just so much work to be done in our world. It's good to celebrate ALL the workers.

So thank you and good night.

School daze . . .

Tonight would be a good night to IMAGINE . . . to sit up with the pillows propped behind the back and "just pretend" to be sitting at a school desk. . . .

I know I am supposed to sit up straight and pay attention and do what the teacher tells me to do. I rode here on a big yellow school bus, and I have a lunch box and some books and pencils and crayons. I wonder what I will learn today. Will we read a story about dinosaurs or draw a picture of a volcano or talk about elephants? Will we go on a field trip to an aquarium where they have those big fish or to a museum where we will learn about paintings and artists? There are SOOO many new things to learn every day—even when my "school" is in my own house!

Dear God, I'm glad you surprise me with new things to learn every day. It's good to go to school to learn, and it's good to learn things at home too. When I get big, I will probably go to college, and when I graduate, I will know LOTS of things. But there is one thing I will never learn EVERYTHING about—and that is YOU!

So thank you and good night.

Give me s'more...

Tonight would be a good night to IMAGINE . . .
to make the covers into a tent and "just pretend"
to be on a camping trip. . . .

It's not easy putting up a tent in the woods,
but we did it, and I think it will be fun to sleep in
a tent tonight. Now we are going for a walk in the
woods and the leaves are crunching under our
feet and falling on our heads because it is time for

all the leaves to leave the trees. When we get back from the walk, we are going to have a fire and sit around telling spooky stories and roasting hot dogs and THEN . . . hot dog! . . . best of all . . . we are going to roast marshmallows and make some s'mores with graham crackers and chocolate. Who could ask for anything s'more!

Dear God, I like crunching through the leaves. Sometimes I pick up a pile of leaves and look at them and trace around a few of them on a piece of paper. And you know what? Each tree has a different kind of leaf! But I guess you knew that since you made the trees and leaves. I love this time of year because of the way the leaves turn different colors and because it's the time when we get to roast hot dogs and marshmallows outdoors.

So thank you and good night.

Trick or treat! . . .

Tonight would be a good night to IMAGINE . . . to get under the covers and curl up into a round ball and "just pretend" to be a round jack-o-lantern. . . .

Somebody sat me here on the front porch on Halloween night and I like being here because I can see allll up and down the street and see who is coming. Here comes somebody now. Ohh . . . it's a little girl who looks just like a pretty princess— and her friend has a long furry tail and whiskers painted on her face and keeps saying "meow." Oh, oh, here comes a strange bunch . . . one has a green face and green hair that stands straight up, one has a red face and red horns on his head, and the other has a white sheet draped over her with big black eyes painted on the sheet. What kind of kids are these anyway? They're all giggling and laughing and taking candy from that nice lady at the front door—and some of them don't even say thank you. Don't they know how to be polite like I do? I just sit here and SMILE at everybody.

Dear Lord, Halloween is a lot of fun and I like to dress up and make believe I'm something or somebody else. And I like to see how my friends dress up too. But please help us all remember to watch for cars and be careful and be polite and ALWAYS say thank you for the treats. Oh, and, Lord, I'm glad you gave us pumpkin patches with big fat pumpkins so we can have pumpkin pies—and jack-o-lanterns too!

So thank you and good night.

Invisible me . . .

Tonight would be a good night to IMAGINE . . . to sink my whole body down under the covers and "just pretend" to be invisible. . . .

Here I am—but nobody knows it. I'm invisible. I could pick up a cookie and carry it across the kitchen and people would think the cookie was leaving the room by itself! I could listen in on conversations and no one would know I heard what they said. I could change the TV channel in the middle of a program and everyone would think the TV was acting crazy. So what WILL I do? Do I really WANT to sneak cookies and eavesdrop and annoy people?

Well, MAYBE I do sometimes. But if I was invisible, how could anyone play ball with me—or find me to give me a hug? I guess being visible is better than being INvisible.

Dear Lord, sometimes I DO feel invisible. I do something right or polite or nice—and nobody sees me do it. Nobody notices or says thank you. It's like I was invisible. But then I make a mistake—and EVERYBODY sees me. EVERYBODY is mad at me. Well, maybe that's not quite right, Lord. When I do something good, YOU see me. You know. And when I make a mistake but say I'm sorry, you forgive me. I'm glad you notice, Lord.

So thank you and good night.

Choo choo and clickety-clack...

Tonight would be a good night to IMAGINE . . . to look out the window and "just pretend" to be on a train. . . .

I am sitting by the train window so I can look out and watch all the things we pass by. I have my train ticket. I have my backpack. I didn't forget anything. Now the conductor is calling, "Alllaboaard!" People standing outside are waving goodbye to me. Now the train is starting to rumble along the tracks . . . choo, choo . . . chugga, chugga . . . clickety clack, clickety clack. Now the train is going faster and faster and I can hear its whistle blowing . . . wooooweee . . .

woooooweee . . . I like to hear that sound. I remember once I heard a train whistle somewhere and thought it would be fun to be riding on a train—and now I am!

Dear Lord, it's fun to play the train game. I can pretend to be the conductor who takes up tickets or the engineer who runs the train or the passenger who rides along. When I look at a train, Lord, I see that all the parts of the train work together. The engine pulls a car full of people and that pulls a car full of ponies or pelicans and that pulls a car full of kangaroos or kazoos—and they all chug along together. That's the way people are supposed to work together, isn't it, Lord? Grownups and kids, friends and family. Help us remember to work together, Lord.

So thank you and good night.

Pilgrims and pumpkins ...

Tonight would be a good night to IMAGINE . . . to lie very straight and "just pretend" to be a very proper pilgrim. . . .

In my pilgrim family, the men stand very straight and wear black suits with white collars and tall black hats that have big buckles on the front. The women wear long dresses with white aprons and soft white hats. I like to play with some neighbors who wear moccasins and clothes made of animal skins. Some of them wear feathers in their hair—and I LIKE that. We are all getting ready for a big feast. The men went into the forest and shot some wild turkeys. The women roasted the turkeys and yumm . . . those turkeys smell delicious. I helped bring in some big orange pumpkins from the field and they got chopped up and mixed up with brown sugar and spices and made into pumpkin pies. And our friends are bringing corn and other good things they grew in the fields. We will feast together and be thankful for a good harvest. And I will be really thankful if I get a turkey drumstick!

Dear God, I think the pilgrims had a great idea to have a big feast with their family and friends in thanksgiving for all the good things they had in this new country. I'm glad we still have a Thanksgiving Day in America. And I know we have so many MORE good things than the pilgrims did—so please help us all to remember to say a thanksgiving prayer before EVERY meal, EVERY day.

So thank you and good night.

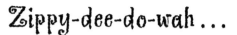

Zippy-dee-do-wah...

Tonight would be a good night to IMAGINE . . . to put my feet together, to put my hands together, to lie very straight and "just pretend" to be zipped up in a sleeping bag. . . .

I feel all snug and safe, zipped up in a bag! And now I wonder who ever came up with such a good idea. I can zip it up, with just my head peeking out, and feel like I'm a spy hiding behind a bush or a big black bear hibernating for the winter. I could take my sleeping bag camping—or just outside in my backyard—and I could look up at the stars in the night and feel like the pilot of a jet plane zooming through the sky or maybe like an angel flying around to watch over the world. And when I'm in a sleeping bag, I don't have to worry about the covers falling off my bed!

Dear God, sometimes I don't want to go to bed at night but I know I SHOULD—so I can get enough sleep to store up lots of energy for tomorrow. And besides, it can be fun to be in a nice comfy bed—or in a zip-up sleeping bag—because nighttime is the only time I can go flying with the stars.

So thank you and good night.

On the shelf . . .

Tonight would be a good night to IMAGINE . . . to put my hands down and pull my knees up and "just pretend" to be a teddy bear sitting on a shelf. . . .

I've been sitting here on the shelf all week—waiting for somebody to play with me. Nobody has even noticed how lonely I am. Don't they know I want to be with somebody? I want to sit in somebody's lap or sit on the sofa or even sit on the floor. I just want to be somewhere besides this shelf. The train went out to play. The doll left the room. The truck rolled out. The action figures all went out together. But here I sit. Oh yes, I know . . . maybe it was somebody else's turn. I HAVE gone out a lot before. I have been along on lots of fun family times—to take a ride in the car or to go to church or even on vacations. But now, here I am, all sad and lonely—just sitting on the shelf, just waiting for somebody to give me a hug.

Dear Jesus, sometimes I get lonely too and need somebody to give me a hug. Sometimes I feel selfish because I know I have lots of toys and I have gone to lots of nice places with my parents and THEY need some time to do things without me. But sometimes they get SO busy, they don't have time to play with me, and I feel like they've forgotten all about me. I don't want to get in anybody's way or take up too much of anybody's time, but please, dear Jesus, remind my family that kids need time too, kids get lonely too. Kids need lots of hugs.

So thank you and good night.

Once upon a time...

Tonight would be a good night to IMAGINE . . . to hold my pillow tight and "just pretend" to be holding the neck of a baby dinosaur. . . .

With my magic time machine, I've traveled back to once upon a time when dinosaurs lived on the earth. When I saw them I was afraid of the big dinosaurs, so I hid in the forest. THEN a baby dinosaur came and found me and wanted to play. I gave the little guy half of the peanut butter sandwich I brought along on the trip, and I guess dinosaurs like peanut butter because after that, we became good friends. We chased each other and played hide-and-seek and leap-frog. But now my time machine is ready for me to go back home, so I am giving my new friend a big hug around the neck to say goodbye.

Dear Jesus, the world must have been VERY different when dinosaurs lived here. I like to THINK about dinosaurs because they look so different from the animals who live on the earth today— but I probably wouldn't like to meet a REAL one. Even a baby dinosaur would probably be too big for me to hug, so I'm glad you let me live now instead of once upon a time. I'm glad I have some stuffed animals I can hug instead. They never growl at me or bite me. And they are nice to hug when it's time to go to sleep.

So thank you and good night.

Wintertime

Snow, Blow, Ho-Ho-Ho Time

Brr ... the polar bear ...

Tonight would be a good night to IMAGINE . . .
to settle down, to get comfy and "just pretend"
to be a fluffy white polar bear. . . .

Polar bears have lots to do. I've been out in the snow all day—working and playing and growling when something happened I didn't like. I went searching for something good to eat . . . taking time out to roll in the snow like a snowball. I saw a rabbit chasing a rabbit. I saw a cloud chasing another cloud. I had fun playing with my bear friends. I made BIIIG footprints and tracks when I walked in the snow. But now I'm tired, so I'm going to snuggle down in my thick fur coat and have a warm winter's sleep.

Dear Jesus, I like to play pretend, but I'm glad I can stop and be ME again. I'm glad I live in a house instead of in the snow. I like to PLAY in the snow with my friends and leave footprints. But when I get cold, I'm glad I can go home and take off my mittens and boots and drink hot chocolate. And I'm also glad I have a nice warm bed where I can snuggle up when I get oh-so-tired and need to rest.

So thank you and good night.

Who's in that igloo?...

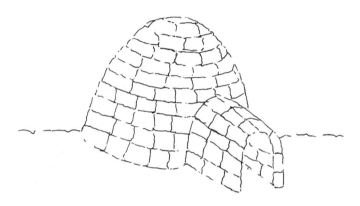

Tonight would be a good night to IMAGINE . . . to get covered up real warm and then "just pretend" to be an eskimo on the way to an igloo. . . .

Snow here, snow there, snow everywhere . . . but I'm warm in my heavy fur-lined jacket with the big hood that fits all around my face. I'm wearing snow shoes that look like big tennis rackets, and it's hard to trudge my way through the deep snow with tennis racket feet. But soon I'll be back at the igloo where my family and I will have fish for dinner and then settle down for the night. My igloo is made of snow and ice, but it's still a warm home for the winter. In the summer, we'll probably move to a tent made of animal skins, but tonight we'll snuggle down in our fur blankets. We may even play peekaboo in our igloo!

Dear Jesus, when you were a little boy on earth, you lived where it was warm, so I guess you never got to have snowball fights or make a snowman. But I guess you still know how much fun snow can be. I like to PLAY in the snow, but I'm not sure I'd like to live in a snow house. But maybe the kids who live in igloos wouldn't like to live in MY house! It's good that the world is full of so many different kinds of people and different kinds of houses. I like to learn about all of them and maybe some day I'll travel around and see some of them. But right now, I like MY house the best.

So thank you and good night.

Who, whooo? . . .

Tonight would be a good night to IMAGINE . . . to open my eyes very wide and stretch my arms out like wings and "just pretend" to be a WHO WHO hoot-owl. . . .

It is very dark and I am sitting high on a tree branch and there is nobody else in this dark but me. I know that because I can SEE in the dark and stay awake in the night. I am a big bird with big eyes and I look around my own private dark night and I say

WHO . . . whooo? But wait a minute. It might be FUN to stay awake all night if I could see in the dark! But if I stayed awake all night, in the morning I would be very tired and I would have to sleep all day. If I slept all day, I couldn't play ball or go swimming or do fun things with my friends. I couldn't even have my favorite sandwich for lunch. And I wouldn't ever have anybody to talk to me or laugh with me because when I was awake at night everybody else would be asleep!

Dear Jesus, I'm glad you let the owl stay awake at night and let me stay awake in the day. There are so many things I like to do in the daytime—so many places to go and discover. I guess that's why you made people to sleep and rest at night but taught them to get up in the morning, so they could work and play and have fun in the day.

So thank you and good night.

Blastoff!...

Tonight would be a good night to IMAGINE . . . to lie back with a pillow under my knees so they're higher than my head and "just pretend" to be an astronaut, strapped in and ready for takeoff. . . .

The countdown is almost over . . . the engines are roaring . . . and I'm excited but scared too. What will it be like in space? I've gone to astronaut school, but will I remember what to do when I'm supposed to do it? Oh, oh, here we goooo! I'm punching buttons. I'm talking to Mission Control and listening for instructions coming through the speakers in my helmet. And now we're in space. Instead of being on earth, looking UP at the sky—I'm in the sky looking DOWN at the earth! The world looks so pretty—like a big round ball with green and blue splotches. It's great being an astronaut. It's great being in space. But when I look at the world, all of a sudden, I'm homesick! I want to go home.

Dear Lord, you made the world and you know all about space. You made me and you know all about me. You know that when it's time to GO somewhere new or DO something new, sometimes I'm excited—but scared too. I want to be brave like an astronaut, but sometimes I just want to go home—where it's safe. But that's OK because I know you'll help me grow up to be brave and safe too.

So thank you and good night.

A dark and stormy night...

Tonight would be a good night to IMAGINE . . . to cuddle up warm and snug and "just pretend" it's a very stormy night. . . .

I'm wearing my raincoat and my rain hat and my rubber boots, but I still feel wet because the rain is coming down sooo hard. The wind is blowing and making weird whining sounds that sound like a baby's crying. The trees are bending down and shaking like they're scared. I'M a little bit scared too. I better run fast and get home before the storm gets worse. Whew! I just made it in the door before big bolts of lightning began racing all across the sky and then the loud booming thunder began. It's fun to WATCH a storm, but it's more fun to watch it from the INSIDE than from the OUTSIDE!

Dear God, storms DO scare me sometimes and I know I should NOT stay outside when there's lightning because it can be dangerous. When I watch a storm from inside my window I like to pretend that the lightning comes from YOUR flash camera and you're taking pictures of the world—and the thunder comes from the biggest drum in YOUR brass band and it's playing music for the rain. I'm really glad you made lightning and thunder to go with the rain.

So thank you and good night.

Me and my pillow...

Tonight would be a good night to IMAGINE . . . to fluff up my pillow, to look at my pillow and then to "just pretend" my pillow is NOT a pillow at all. . . .

What will my pillow be tonight? It could be a cloud. It could be a really big blob of cotton candy. It could be a white bunny rabbit. Or it could be a big white monster coming out of a snowdrift, holding out a big fluffy furry paw.

Is it going to use that paw to grab me up and carry me off to its cave—or does it just want to shake hands? Well, I guess it's none of those things. It's just my nice soft friendly pillow that keeps my head comfy every night so I can close my eyes and drift off to dreamland.

Dear Lord, I'm so glad I have a pillow. I've heard that when some people lie down to go to sleep, they like to put their heads on wooden blocks! I wouldn't like that. I like my nice soft pillow. And I know that some people don't have pillows or blankets and some people even have to sleep in cardboard boxes. Please take care of those people tonight, dear Lord. And thank you, because I know I'm really lucky to have a nice place to sleep.

So thank you and good night.

Going underground . . .

Tonight would be a good night to IMAGINE . . .
to crawl under the covers and "just pretend" to
be exploring a cave. . . .

It's very cold and dark in this cave and very
mysterious. It feels funny to know that I am

UNDER the ground. But I'm glad I'm not by myself. I'm with a group and we have a tour guide and she has a big light on her helmet—but when I look in the corners, it is still very dark there. I wonder if a pirate could have left a treasure chest hidden in that corner. I wonder if there are bats hanging from the ceiling in the dark, waiting to swoop down on us. The guide is showing us lots of interesting things about caves and it's fun seeing them and hearing her stories, but I sure hope her light doesn't go out. Just in case, I'm going to hang on tight to a grownup's hand until we get out of here!

Dear God, you sure gave us lots of surprises. When you made the world, you didn't just put exciting things on the earth and in the ocean, you even put strange and wonderful things under the ground in caves. I'm sure glad you have such a great imagination—and I'm glad you gave me a little bit of it too!

So thank you and good night.

Whose birthday is this? ...

Tonight would be a good night to IMAGINE . . . to wrap up in the covers the way a present gets wrapped up and "just pretend" that it's almost time for a birthday party. . . .

It's fun getting ready for a birthday party—inviting friends, blowing up balloons, decorating a cake or cupcakes. If it's somebody else's birthday, I might get to help pick out the present and wrap it up. Now what would I pick out . . . a toy, a computer game, a music CD? But maybe it's MY birthday. That's even MORE fun because I know people will be picking out presents to give ME! But no, it's NOT my birthday. It's a very special birthday, so special that people all over the world will be giving presents AND getting presents. And I will get some too! Why? Because THIS birthday party will be held on Jesus' birthday—on Christmas Day!

Dear Jesus, help me remember that Christmas is not just about Santa Claus going Ho-ho-ho and everybody getting presents. It's YOUR birthday! I don't give presents to other people when it's MY birthday—but lots of people get presents when it's YOUR birthday. I guess that's because you love everybody and YOU give presents EVERY DAY. I know you give ME lots of presents—air to breathe and water to drink, sunshine in the day and stars at night, and a whole WORLD full of things to explore. With you as my friend, EVERY day is like a birthday.

So thank you and good night.

The wise, looong journey . . .

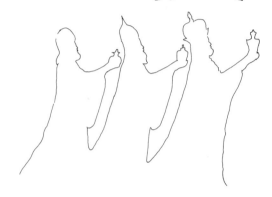

Tonight would be a good night to IMAGINE . . .
to roll up like I'm packed in a duffle bag and "just
pretend" to be on a long journey. . . .

The road is dusty and I have been riding this
camel for a looong time. The camel's name is
Humpty-Bumpty, and he has given me a very
bumpty ride. He doesn't get thirsty very often,
but I do! I get so tired and I wish I had a nice cool
drink and maybe a sandwich, but there are no
ride-in restaurants along the way. When we DO
find a friendly place to stop, we don't stay very
long because we are on an IMPORTANT
journey. My friends and I don't have a map and
we don't have a cell-phone to call and ask for
directions to find where we want to go. But we

DO have a star to follow—a very bright star. We haven't told anyone yet because it is a secret, but we are on our way to find Baby Jesus!

Dear Jesus, tonight I wonder how the Wise Men felt when they got off their camels and met you. When I see the Christmas crib at church with you and Mary and Joseph and the sheep and the camels and the Wise Men, I wonder what I would say to you if I was there on that first Christmas. Even though I can't see you in person now, I'm glad I can always talk to you in my heart and in my head. And that can be our secret, because nobody but you and I will know what we talk about. I'm glad you came to earth so we could learn about you, and I'm glad you are my all-time friend.

So thank you and good night.

Sleeping out or over...

Tonight would be a good night to IMAGINE . . .
to roll up in the covers and "just pretend" to be
at a slumber party. . . .

I wasn't sure what a slumber party was until I
got invited. Then I found out that when somebody invites some friends to come over and
spend the night, that's a slumber party. So here I
am at my friend's house and we are having lots of

fun. There are some other friends here too and we have been playing games and having snacks—and giggling a lot. I think the word "slumber" means sleep, but we are having so much fun, I don't know if we will do much sleeping tonight!

Dear Lord, why is it more fun to sleep out in a tent or over at somebody else's house or maybe in a motel room on vacation? I guess it's fun because it's something different. Every night I get in this same bed and sometimes I don't want to do that, so I pretend I need a drink of water or I want to hear one more story. Sometimes I pretend I am not sleepy yet—but you and I know, Lord, that I really AM sleepy and need to close my eyes. I can't keep them open any longer.

So thank you and good night.

Easy, please-y prayers

... for the nights when you are tooo tired to "just pretend."

Please, dear God, make me brave so I won't be afraid of the dark. I am usually NOT afraid of the dark, but sometimes I am.

Please, Lord, remind me how lucky I am to have eyes and nose, fingers and toes—and friends who give me lots of hellos.

Please, God, help me to know you, to love you, and to serve you—tomorrow and every day.

Please, Jesus, when I don't know how to act, remind me to ask, "What would Jesus do?"—and then do that!

Please, Jesus, help me to remember to try to do what I am TOLD to do even when I WANT to do something different.

Please, Lord, remind me to always say thank you when I get a gift. Even if it's just a little gift or NOT the gift I wanted, teach me to be polite enough to say thanks.

Please, God, help me to NOTICE when someone in my family is sad—so I can try to do something to help change that sad into glad.

Please, Jesus, remind me NOT to leave things in the middle of the floor because people keep falling over them.

Please, Jesus, help me to know when NOT to talk. I know you are not supposed to talk when somebody else is talking, but sometimes I forget.

Please, dear God, remind me to be very good to my grandparents, uncles, aunts, and cousins because they are all part of MY family—and YOUR family.

Please God, help me to TRY to like the vegetables I think are yucky—because they are GOOD for me and I want to be GOOD!

Please, Jesus, remind me to wash my hands, front and back, BEFORE I eat a meal or snack!

Please, dear God, teach me how to pray better. I know I can always just talk to you, but I would like to learn some of the prayers the big people say.

Please, Jesus, let us have more ice cream for dessert. I bet you never got to taste ice cream when you were on earth, so I'll be glad to eat an extra bowl-full for you!

Please, Lord, help me to be brave when I get an ouchie—and help me always remember to get someone to put some medicine and a Band-Aid on it so it won't get worse!

Please, Lord, remind me to always buckle up my seatbelt when I ride in a car—so I won't go flying without wings!

Please, dear Jesus, help me to know how to act when I meet a new kid. I might be embarrassed or scared with someone new— but maybe the other kid feels that way too.

Please, God, send my feet outside if I start to forget that baseball and basketball are OUTSIDE games, not inside games.

Please, dear Jesus, help me to remember to ALWAYS say please—so my family won't have to remind me to do that. Did YOUR mother always have to remind YOU to do that when you were on earth?

Please, Lord, remind me that music is fun, much better than none—but it shouldn't be loud when it's not allowed!

Please, God, help me to drink all my milk and eat all my food—so I'll be the healthiest in the neighborhood!

Please, Lord, help me learn to draw pretty pictures—but never on a wall or hall!

Please, Lord, remind me it's good to share everything—EXCEPT coughs and sneezes!

Please, dear God, help me learn to swim VERY well—and be VERY careful. Water is fun but it CAN be dangerous because you made people to breathe air, not water!

Please, Lord, remind me to thank you for rivers and lakes, flowers and trees, birthday cakes and bumble bees.

Please, God, remind me to look all around me every day and SEE and thank you for all the great things you made in our world— like brown bears and green frogs, tall giraffes and short groundhogs.

Please, dear Jesus, when I sleep or play, all night and all day, be at my side, to teach and guide.

Please, God, excuse me if I get soooo tired some night that I forget to say a nitey-nite prayer. Please know that I still love you and want you to be with me always.

OTHER BOOKS BY
BERNADETTE MCCARVER SNYDER

Have You Ever Seen an Ant Who Can't?

Have You Ever Heard a Catfish Purr?

Have You Ever Heard a Hummingbird Hum?

Have You Ever Seen an Elephant Sneeze?

Painting Rainbows with Broken Crayons